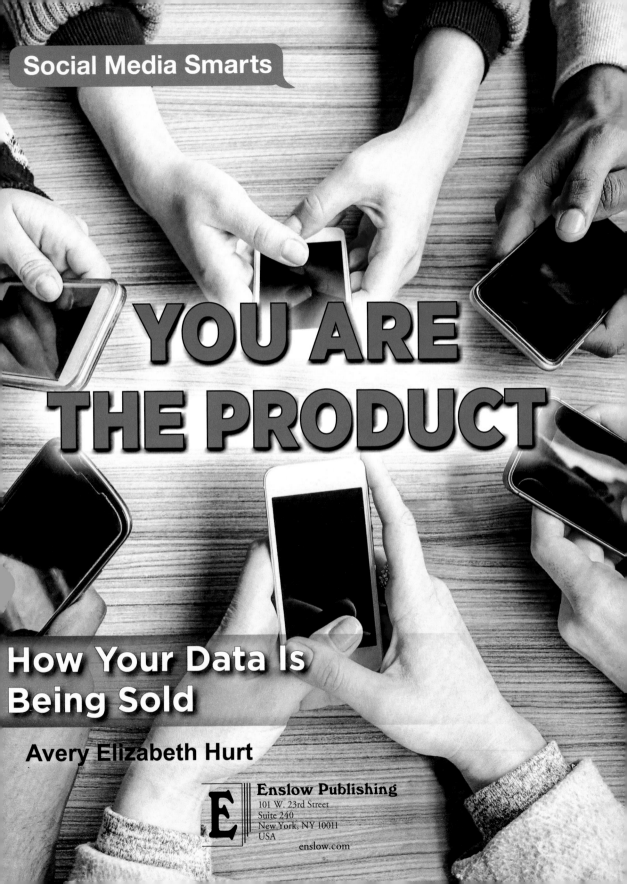

Social Media Smarts

YOU ARE THE PRODUCT

How Your Data Is Being Sold

Avery Elizabeth Hurt

E **Enslow Publishing**
101 W. 23rd Street
Suite 240
New York, NY 10011
USA
enslow.com

Published in 2020 by Enslow Publishing, LLC
101 W. 23rd Street, Suite 240, New York, NY 10011

Library of Congress Cataloging-in-Publication Data

Names: Hurt, Avery Elizabeth, author.
Title: You are the product : how your data is being sold / Avery Elizabeth Hurt.
Description: New York : Enslow Publishing, 2020 | Series: Social media smarts | Audience: Grade level 5-8. | Includes bibliographical references and index.
Identifiers: LCCN 2018057408| ISBN 9781978507814 (library bound) | ISBN 9781978507807 (pbk.)
Subjects: LCSH: Social media—Juvenile literature. | Computer security—Juvenile literature. | Identity theft—Juvenile literature. | Big data—Juvenile literature.
Classification: LCC HM742 .H867 2020 | DDC 302.23/1—dc23
LC record available at https://lccn.loc.gov/2018057408

Printed in the United States of America

To Our Readers: We have done our best to make sure all website addresses in this book were active and appropriate when we went to press. However, the author and the publisher have no control over and assume no liability for the material available on those websites or on any websites they may link to. Any comments or suggestions can be sent by email to customerservice@enslow.com.

Photo Credits: Cover, p. 1 Akhenaton Images/Shutterstock.com; p. 5 Rawpixel.com/Shutterstock.com; p. 6 Vasin Lee/Shutterstock.com; p. 9 Getty Images; p. 11 Alexey Boldin/Shutterstock.com; p. 13 Sam72/Shutterstock.com; p. 16 Profit_Image/Shutterstock.com; p. 18 PR Image Factory/Shutterstock.com; p. 21 Tetiana Yurchenko/Shutterstock.com; p. 24 © iStockphoto.com/tomch; p. 28 Mila Supinskaya Glashchenko/Shutterstock.com; p. 32 karelnoppe/Shutterstock.com; pp. 33, 37 Sasin Paraksa/Shutterstock.com; p. 35 Trum Ronnarong/Shutterstock.com; p. 41 Syda Productions/Shutterstock.com.

Contents

Introduction

If you're like most people these days, you're rarely more than an arm's length away from your smartphone. You get up in the morning and check to see if you missed any texts or emails while you were asleep. Then you check Instagram, Snapchat, Facebook, Tumblr, and any other social media sites where you have an account. Then, and only then, do you go to the bathroom, brush your teeth, and grab some breakfast.

On the way to school, you listen to music on YouTube. You check your feeds at lunch and in-between classes. If you can get away with it, you take quick peeks during the less exciting parts of classes. Social media is part of your life. It's how you stay in touch with friends. It's how you find out what's going on around town and in your social group. It's where you express yourself, and where you have your say.

If this more or less describes you, you're not alone. According to the Pew Research center, ninety-five percent of American teens either have a smartphone or have access to one. Forty-five percent say that they are online "almost constantly."[1]

Whether you're aware of it or not, you give a great deal of information to these sites, both in your public posts, and in the details of your account. Your favorite social media providers know where you are and where you're planning to go. They know who your friends are and who you've just had a spat with. They know what school you attend and what grade you are in. They also know things such as what kinds of clothes you like to wear, your favorite soft drink, what movies you watch, what books you read, what politicians you support. (And they know which ones you think are totally full of it.)

These days just about everybody uses a smartphone to stay in touch with friends, keep up with the news, and get informed.

People often aren't aware just how much data they keep on their phones—and how extremely valuable their data is to many companies.

These may seem like trivial facts—and taken in isolation, they are. But gather enough of that kind of data, and you can piece together an amazingly accurate picture of a person. But so what? Other than your friends and family, who cares what you had for lunch or what concert you're going to this weekend?

As it turns out, a lot of people care. And they're willing to pay big bucks for the information.

Have you ever wondered how social media companies make money? What do they sell? What is their product? Most users haven't. But it's a good question. The way these companies make money is by selling targeted advertising. And those advertisers base decisions about whom to target by analyzing lots and lots of information about people who use media—this is called user data. Advertisers pay social media providers, and what they pay for is information about social media users. So what is the product Snapchat and Instagram and Facebook are offering?

You are that product.

This book will explain the mysterious workings of targeted advertising and how social media uses your data to make money. By knowing how all this works, you can do a better job of protecting your personal information and learn to use your favorite sites with more confidence.

Who Am I?

In April 2018, Mark Zuckerberg, founder and CEO of Facebook, testified before the United States Senate. He explained to the senators that Facebook's mission was to connect people around the world. In order to do that, the service would always be free. Senator Orrin Hatch wanted to know how that was possible. Hatch asked, "How do you sustain a business model in which users don't pay for your service?" Zukerberg smiled at the 84-year-old legislator and said, "Senator, we run ads."[1]

Hatch's question was not as naive as Zuckerberg made it sound. And Zuckerberg's answer was not quite as straightforward as it sounded, either.

As Zuckerberg explained, Facebook and almost all social media companies sell advertising space on their sites. Businesses then post advertisements there. The social media sites use the income they get for these ads to pay the costs of operating their businesses. Users don't have to pay a cent.

This is not a new business model. Most media outlets, including newspapers, television, and radio stations work this way, too. They always have. The money subscribers pay for

Facebook chairman and CEO Mark Zuckerberg testifies before a combined Senate Judiciary and Commerce committee hearing on Capitol Hill on April 10, 2018.

newspapers or cable packages is not nearly enough to pay the costs of providing these services. So, like Facebook, they run ads. Take a televised baseball game, for example. From time to time, the game pauses and viewers see an advertisement for pizza, pick-up trucks, or cell phone service. Viewers "pay" to watch the game by being willing to watch the ad. (Of course, on television, you can pop into the kitchen for a snack while the ads are on.) The companies who buy time (called "spots") during television or radio broadcasts foot the bill so viewers can watch for free. Advertisers hope that enough viewers will be persuaded to buy what they are selling to make back the cost of the advertisements. Getting a chance to put their messages before the millions of people watching the game is worth a lot of money to these companies. Zuckerberg told Hatch that Facebook worked the same way.

But he didn't fully answer the senator's question. The emergence of the internet has taken the practice of selling ads to an entirely new level.

Getting to Know You

Advertisers have always wanted to know as much as possible about their target audiences. Think of an old-fashioned print newspaper, for example. Once you turn past the first page news and get beyond the editorials, you'll start to see advertisements for local businesses: flower shops, restaurants, grocery stores. The businesses who buy ad space in a local paper know that their message will reach the people most likely to be their customers: people who live in their town.

Television programs and national magazines have wider audiences. For a television network or magazine to sell ads, the company has to provide potential advertisers with as much information as they can gather about their readers and viewers. They learn all they can about their readers or viewers and compile a composite profile. For example, the magazine

Six Degrees of Social Media

Facebook dominates the social media world. As of 2018, it had more than one billion daily users. Instagram isn't far behind with more than a billion monthly users. Snapchat and Tumblr are nipping at their heels. But when it comes to social media, all of these companies are new kids on the block—even Facebook. The first social media site was founded in 1996. It was called Six Degrees. That was a reference to a concept called six degrees of separation. It was the idea that any individual is never more than six connections away from any other individual. It was a great name for a social network. Millions of people signed up. But the service didn't really catch on. It was shut down in 2000.

Other similar networks came along, such as LiveJournal, Friendster, and MySpace. But when Facebook got rolling, everyone else had to take a back seat. Analysts don't agree on why Facebook has been so much more successful than other similar sites. But there's no doubt that it is. Facebook is a household word.

Social media is not so new. People have been using a variety of websites to keep in touch with friends and family since the 1990s.

National Geographic Kids describes its typical reader as a ten-year-old boy whose favorite subject is science.[2] He reads mysteries and books about animals. He loves to impress his friends with weird-but-true facts. The business magazine *Forbes* describes its typical reader as a man in his forties who earns over a hundred thousand dollars a year.[3] There's not much overlap in those two groups.

On the internet, however, things aren't so simple. A person who signs into a social media site could be from anywhere in the world. The ages, tastes, interests, and needs of these people vary considerably. A company could go broke trying to find the best place to post its ads. But that's not a problem. Advertisers now have a great new way to find their perfect customers.

How Do They Know That?

You may have noticed that some ads seem to follow you around the internet. And the ads are creepily relevant. You're on the tennis team and you see lots of advertisements for rackets. Your friend doesn't play tennis but is an amateur photographer. And guess what? He sees loads of ads for cameras. When you sign on to Facebook, you see ads for things a teenager might be interested in. When your mother signs on, she sees completely different ads. You've probably never seen a Facebook ad for vacation property or investment consulting. Your grandparents rarely see ads for video

Ads on websites can be terribly annoying. But that's often how content providers pay the bills. Without them content wouldn't be free.

games. How do advertisers manage to serve you ads that are so perfect for you? These advertisers know a great deal about you.

How is this different from the reader profiles magazines offer their advertisers? For one thing, your social media profile is a lot more detailed. *National Geographic Kids* and *Forbes* describes their typical readers in very general terms. But when you sign onto Snapchat, Instagram, or Facebook, or even when you're just cruising the web, the websites you visit know more about you than just a general profile. They may know even more about you than your neighbors do. Media outlets—especially social media outlets—no longer have to make guesses about what their users are like. Users tell them! Or at the very least leave a trail of clues.

All of this information is called Big Data. And it's really fascinating how they gather it.

What Do They Want?

Shelly is fourteen years old and lives in Hampton, Virginia. She has a cat named Sparky. She loves to play video games and is very good at it. She's point guard for the Mustangs, her school's basketball team. Her favorite soft drink is Fizzy Lizzy, pineapple flavor. She also drinks a lot of herbal tea. She's very bright, but sometimes struggles in school. Her parents are Republicans, but Shelly doesn't have much interest in politics. She collects figurines of horses and funky candles. She has a crush on a guy named Hal.

Right now, *at this very moment,* Shelly is walking home from a friend's house. The friend is Amy. Amy is almost fifteen and loves . . .

Big data knows all this—and more. Shelly and Amy aren't real people, but if they were big data would know about them because big data knows about almost everybody.

It's Like Me to Like You

Every time you go online, you leave an electronic trail. When you visit a website, small text files called cookies are placed on your computer, tablet, or smartphone. This is a kind of identification that allows the site to recognize you when you come back. By tracking these cookies, someone can see what sites you visit, what pages you visit on those sites, how long you stay, and so on.

Your electronic trail is like a set of digital footprints that tell the story of where you've been, when you were there, and how long you stayed.

When you visit a social media site, that trail is far more detailed and rich. There are dozens of social media sites, but because it's by far the biggest, let's talk about Facebook. When you are active on Facebook, you share a lot of details about yourself. Sometimes that's obvious. You share news about your favorite sports team. You post a picture of yourself accepting a track and field award. You share memes about how cats are smarter than dogs. It doesn't take a mathematical genius to figure out that you are a Red Sox fan who runs cross country and owns a cat. Anyone taking a close look at your social media feeds can see that. After all, that's part of the reason you post this information. That's why it's called *social* media and not *private* media. You want your friends to know you. But you are probably sharing far more information than you realize. And you're not just giving it to your friends.[1]

Take your "likes," for example. Say a post strikes your fancy on Facebook or Instagram. You give it a "thumbs up" or click the heart icon. You may "like" the post because it's funny. You may agree with the sentiment or want to support a cause. You may just want to give a friend some recognition for a cool comment. It's not something you spend hours thinking about. You click and move on. Then there are apps and games. Have you ever taken a quiz on a social media site? What Hogwarts house do you belong to? Which *Star Wars* character are you? Are you an introvert or an extrovert? These aren't serious personality tests. No single detail provided by your likes, posts, or answers to surveys and quizzes reveal much about you. But when studied with the right scientific tools, they can say a lot.

Now and Later

A branch of science called data analytics uses statistics, mathematics, and psychology to sort through huge amounts

People who work in data analysis have engaging and challenging jobs. The market for data analysts is likely to continue to grow.

of data to find patterns. Data scientists combine and compare your data with similar information from millions of other people. This gives them a remarkably good picture of who you are. By simply analyzing what you "like" on Facebook, scientists can determine your age, gender, sexual orientation, and ethnicity. They can tell if you are conservative or liberal and if you use drugs. They can tell if you are intelligent and whether or not you are happy. They can do this with upwards of 80 percent accuracy. You are no longer a theoretical person, like the boy who reads *National Geographic Kids* magazine. The profile is getting much more specific.

Data analysis can determine what you are like now. It can also make predictions about what you will do in the future.

A Social Career?

If all this talk of computer models and algorithms is exciting, you might want to consider preparing for a career in data analysis. A degree in data analysis can lead to a well-paying and fun job. Technology companies hire a lot of data analysts. But they aren't the only companies that need them. Insurance companies, health care organizations, banks, and government agencies make use of data analysis, too. Computer science and mathematics classes are a good place to start honing your skills. When you get to college, you can major in mathematics or computer science. But your choices aren't that limited. Many data analysts have degrees in finance or economics. It's a job that can pay the bills while feeding your inner geek.

This is called predictive analysis. Scientists use computer algorithms and sometimes artificial intelligence to make these predictions. Data about how you've behaved in the past is fed into a mathematical model. The model looks for trends and patterns in your past behavior. It also looks at the past behavior of many other people who are similar to you in key ways. Based on all this information, this model can predict how you are likely to respond in the future. For example, it may predict that you are not very likely to download the next Jesse McCartney song. It might predict which colleges you are likely to apply to.[2]

The social media networks you use have tons of data about you. And that data belongs to them. As Zuckerberg said to Senator Hatch, "We run ads." What he did not say was that Facebook (and similar companies) collect troves of data about their users. Then they use this data to help their real customers target those users with their messages. Those messages might be anything from ads for athletic shoes to reminders to vote. The good news about all this is that businesses are happy to pay to advertise on these sites. That means you don't have to pay to use them. And if you're going to have to see ads, you might as well see ads that might be useful to you. Targeted advertising means you don't have to sit through pitches for pick-up trucks if you aren't even old enough to drive. At the same time, you're likely to be one of the first to hear about a new video game you'll probably love.

Big data allows companies to carefully filter the information that shows up on your computer in order to perfectly target you and your interests.

The bad news is that you may not be comfortable with these big companies collecting data about you. If that's the case, there are things you can do to limit how much they collect. But before we get into that, let's talk about who is collecting this information. The people interested in your data aren't just retailers.

3

Who Are They?

●●●

So far we've been talking about advertising. But personal information about social media users is useful for plenty of other reasons, too. This information is so valuable that entire companies are built around collecting, analyzing, and selling this data. And like most valuable things, some people steal it.

Have We Met?

Data brokers are companies that collect, analyze, and sell data on just about everybody. You have a business relationship with the social media sites you use. You sign up for an account. You agree to the terms of service. You don't have a business relationship with data brokers. You sign no user agreements. You don't volunteer to give them facts about your life. This is the kind of information we talked about in the last chapter—who you are, how old you are, where you live, what you buy, and much more.

These companies get this information from many different places. Much of it comes from public records. Birth certificates, driver's licenses, and marriage licenses are all public records. Posts on some social media sites are public. Other information is easy to get as well. Online or catalog purchases, purchases using loyalty cards, and Google searches all leave a trail of information about you. Stores and websites often sell user information to data brokers.

Data broker companies, such as Acxiom and Datalogix, scoop up as much of this information as they can. Then they use powerful computer programs to sort through it and

In many cases, data brokers don't even have to buy information about you. It's already a matter of public record.

organize it. This gives them a profile of what you are like. It may be quite accurate—or wildly inaccurate. In either case, the information is worth a lot of money. Advertisers spend some serious cash for this information. But selling you stuff isn't the only use for this data. Banks can use this information to determine how credit-worthy you are. Insurance companies can use it to get an idea if you're likely to wreck your car. Medical insurance companies can determine if you're at risk for certain diseases or drug addiction. In the 2012 US election, data companies determined if people were Democrats or Republicans by using this kind of information. This allowed the campaigns to better target their ads. Colleges are increasingly using big data to make admissions decisions.[1] Data brokers may not sell your data to anyone who plans to use it for illegal purposes. But your data is only as safe as the security systems of the sites that have it. If the computers of a data broker (or a social media site) get hacked, your data can be stolen. Criminals love to get their hands on this information. This rich trove of data can make it easier for someone to guess your passwords to other sites. This sort of data is often sold on the black market. People can use this information for identity theft, a crime that can involve applying for credit cards in other people's names.

Data brokers have been around for decades. Until recently no one paid them much attention.

I Couldn't Agree More

If you're like most people, you hit the "Agree" button without bothering to read the user agreement. And who could blame you? The things are usually long, boring, and written in difficult-to-understand legal language. According to one study, it would take the average American 250 hours a year to read all of their user contracts. That's more than ten full days a year (if you don't take time to sleep!). Who has time for that? Besides, it's not like you can renegotiate your contract with Snapchat.

Still, it would be nice if user agreements were easier to understand. Who knows what rights you may be giving away when you blindly click "Agree." One idea is to hold tech companies to certain professional standards, like doctors and lawyers must adhere to. Meanwhile it's probably a good idea to at least scan the agreements. Pay especially close attention to the sections that mention what the site can do with your data.

Wake-Up Call

Before the 2016 presidential election, very few people had heard of data brokers. But events in 2016 and 2017 put them in the headlines. Suddenly everyone was learning about data brokers. And what they were learning was troubling.

In 2016, Donald Trump hired a consulting firm to help with his presidential campaign. Political campaigns do this routinely, though the public is rarely interested in the details. But this company was different. It was called Cambridge Analytica, and claimed to be able to be able to take big data to a new level. It offered what it called "psychographic data" on potential voters. Psychographic data goes beyond who you are and what kinds of products you are likely to buy. It attempts to understand your interests, attitudes, even your hopes and dreams.

The consulting firm promised the Trump campaign that it could identify people who might be persuaded to vote for Trump. It also promised that it could tell the campaign exactly what messages would be most likely to convince these people. (These messages would then be delivered via advertisements, Facebook posts, or emails.)

Targeting voters was nothing new; however, this level of targeting was. In order to make good on their promises, Cambridge Analytica developed a personality quiz application for Facebook users. (You knew we'd get back to social media eventually, didn't you?) The quiz app was called "This Is My Digital Life."

The app gathered a tremendous amount of data on the users who agreed to take the quiz. In addition to names and locations, it collected likes, posts, and even direct messages. But it didn't stop there. Quiz takers also agreed to let the app see information on their Facebook "friends." In the end, data on 87 million Facebook users was gathered by this

If people want safe social media where they own and control their information, they may have to come up with creative solutions on their own.

app. The data was given to Cambridge Analytica to use in targeting voters.[2]

Facebook does not sell information about its users to data brokers. (Depending on your privacy settings, data brokers can see a great deal of your information anyway.) However, Facebook does allow researchers to access the data for academic research. That's why Facebook approved this app. They did not, however, approve of it being shared with a political consulting firm. Nonetheless, it was. Facebook banned the quiz in 2015. But by that time, it was too late for millions of users.

This incident attracted the attention of the public to data brokers in general. For the first time, people became aware of just how much information was being collected about them. And more troubling, they became aware of just how easily their data could be misused. Most of the people whose data was shared with Cambridge Analytica did not agree to have it shared. They didn't even know it had been collected. It was a huge scandal for Facebook. It was a huge wake-up call for the public who trusted them with their information.

People are now asking what they can do to protect their online privacy. How can they keep ownership of their own data. There are things you can do. And the good news is that it's much easier if you start while you're young.

Protect Yourself

Much of the problem of data privacy is out of the individual's control. But there is a lot you can do to limit how much of your data is available to data brokers.

Wrong!

These days, people are much more aware of how much data is being collected about them. The Facebook/Cambridge Analytica scandal got a lot of people's attention. Facebook and other sites—Google was one—have started letting users see (at least) some of the information they have on them. A few data brokers will let you know if they have info on you and what they have. When they checked this out, many people found that much of the information was way off.[1] A data broker might have you still listed at an old address. It might say that a forty-year old accountant who rides a mountain bike every weekend is a retiree with heart trouble. A teen who is the president of the student government is flagged as an art teacher.

It's easy to see how this can happen. The mountain biker may have been searching the web for health information for his father. The teen might have looked up portraits online for a school project. It's easy for information to get scrambled. It is a little reassuring when you find that the information is mostly wrong. They may know you, but they don't know you all that well. But that can be a big problem, too. Colleges checking out prospective students or scholarship applicants might get the wrong idea. When you try to get insurance for your first car, you might find that the insurance company has you all wrong. So it's a tricky problem. We wish they didn't collect this stuff. But if they *are* going to collect it, we wish they'd get it right.

The most accurate data comes from places that know you well—social media sites and online retailers, such as Amazon. But data miners vacuum up everything they get. The best first step to protect yourself is to limit what they can get.

Control Your Story

The most effective way to protect your data and your online privacy is to go offline completely: cancel all your social media accounts, dump your email account, and never again Google anything at all. In fact, just give your computer away. Always pay with cash, don't do online banking, and never sign up for rewards programs or similar promotions.

Of course, that's ridiculous. That's the twenty-first-century equivalent of going to the mountains and living alone in a cave. You'll be happy to know that you don't have to go anywhere that far. There's a lot you can do to protect your data and your

Playing Tag

Facial recognition software may be one of the wildest things social media has introduced. It's that little box that pops up on your photos to help you "tag" friends and family members. It's useful. But is it worth it? Outside of social media the software can be dangerous. It's not accurate enough yet to prevent mistakes. For example, when law enforcement agencies use it to identify suspects, it's easy to finger the wrong person.

On the other hand, when used on social media, the technology might actually help protect privacy. If photo recognition is enabled on Facebook, for example, the company can notify you if someone tags you in a photo. If you aren't happy about that, you can ask to have the tag removed. You'll also be notified if someone uses your photo as a profile picture. This is a good way to prevent people using your identity to put up posts. Like so many things on social media, there are pros and cons. But many people prefer to keep their faces private, too.

Facial recognition software is still in its early stages. It's still not very good at recognizing the faces of people of certain ethnic groups.

privacy without giving up the conveniences and joys of the modern age. And the *really* good news is that this is easier to do if you start when you're young.

Here are some fundamentals: Pay attention to privacy policies on your social media accounts. Check these occasionally to make sure nothing has changed. Make your settings as private as you can make them. There's no reason anyone except your friends and family need to see your posts. Be sure and look for "opt-out" buttons and boxes. These buttons and boxes are provided when the site automatically collects information about

Website privacy settings and computer security features are more important now than ever before. Smart users keep them up to date.

you, but gives you the option to say, "no thanks." For example, on Facebook you have to go to your privacy settings and "opt out" of facial recognition.[2] Otherwise, they'll be scanning photos and crowd shots for your face. Settings and options vary a lot from site to site. It can take a little time, but go to each one, find their privacy and security sections, and make sure you have it set up the way you want it.

Be especially careful with third-party apps. These are games, quizzes, and other features that aren't created by the social media site you're on. Other companies (not you, not the site, but another "third party") put them on the site for you to use. They'll often have different rules and practices. Many of them exist mostly, if not solely, to gather data about social media users. If you use any of these, be sure to carefully read the user agreements and opt out of any data sharing. Be suspicious of giveaways and surveys wherever you see them. They are almost always attempts to get information about you. Also, turn off location settings. This not only protects your privacy, it can keep you safe, too. It's never a good idea to announce to strangers where you're hanging out.

Don't Give It Away

Any time any website, app, or social media site asks for personal information about you, beware. Ask yourself "Why do they want this info?" "Why would they *need* it?" A weather app might legitimately need your location to let you know if storms

It's easy to find out who you are, where you are, and what you are doing by tracking your online posts and comments.

are headed your way. Most apps don't need to know where you are all the time—if ever.

Also, be very careful about what you post. You're spending a lot of time trying to protect this information, don't turn around and give it away! If you upload videos to YouTube, select "private," and invite only the people you want to see it. And be respectful of your friend's and family's privacy as well.

If you do all this, your data still won't be perfectly protected. These measures can help a lot, though. However, if users keep demanding change in the way their data is being handled, the future of data privacy might be very different.

The Future of Privacy

●●●

Social media has become so much a part of our lives, it's hard to imagine life without it. It's a relatively new way of communicating, though, and it's still growing and changing. Companies that advertise on social media are still working out the best ways to target their ideal customers. Individual users are still deciding how much privacy they are willing to give up. And the companies that run social media sites are in the middle—trying to plan for the future of their businesses.

The End of Social Media?

According to the Pew Research Center, the boom in social media may be over. After many years of steady growth, the company's data suggests that, as of fall of 2018, use of the popular platforms has leveled off.[1] Does this mean social media is dying? Not at all. It probably just means that all of the people who want to be on social media and can afford the necessary devices are already there.

However, that doesn't mean the public's concerns about privacy aren't causing these companies trouble. Facebook's

Cambridge Analytica scandal (and a more recent breach that exposed still more user data) shook users' trust in the site. The facts the scandal revealed about how most social media sites make money may have damaged public trust in the whole idea of social media. People had once seen social media as a free and easy way to connect with friends. Some used it as a way to keep up with breaking news. Then suddenly, it began to look like a big racket to collect tons of personal data for a profit. American journalist Ari Melber put it like this: "[Facebook's] priorities revolve around profiting off their users...They claim to treat users as customers, or even a 'community,' but as many tech experts have shown, the customers are actually the product."[2] And this is the business

model of virtually all social media sites. It can hurt to realize that you

Rather than leaving social media, many people are demanding government oversight of the world's huge media companies.

aren't a community after all, but instead are a product in a very big business.

It turns out that social media isn't free. You pay with your data. That realization might be enough to make users take their business and their data elsewhere. But where? Few people are willing to give up on social media. They just want a safer, more transparent, and ultimately more private way of connecting with others online. Is that too much to ask?

Maybe not.

Demands for Change

Tim Cook is CEO of Apple, a large multinational technology company. He has spoken out for stronger privacy protections in the tech world. In October 2018, he spoke at a conference of international data protection and privacy commissioners. He carefully outlined the situation:

> Every day, billions of dollars change hands and countless decision are made on the basis of our likes and dislikes, our friends and families, our relationships and conversations, our wishes and fears, our hopes and dreams. These scraps of data—each one harmless enough on their own—are carefully assembled, synthesized, traded and sold. Taken to its extreme, this process creates an enduring digital profile and lets companies know you better than you may know yourself.[3]

Then Cook expressed strong support for passing federal privacy laws in the United States. He said, "We will never achieve technology's true potential without the full faith and confidence of the people who use it." [4] Cook is not alone. (He may be the lone voice in the tech industry, though). More and more people are joining the call for data protection—and not just leaders. Individuals are speaking up, too. Americans are telling Congress that they're concerned about their privacy. If you're worried about this issue, you can have a say, too. Even if you aren't old enough to vote, you are old enough to express an opinion. It's important for legislators to know the concerns of people who will be affected tomorrow by legislation passed (or not passed) today. It won't be too long before you will be able to vote.

You can also demand corporate responsibility from the companies you do business with. If you don't like what social media sites are doing with your data, let them know. You are the product, not the customer. You're crucial to the whole enterprise. Without you, social media sites would have nothing to sell. It's your business those advertisers want.

A Better Idea

Data privacy laws would require businesses to let you know what they do with your data. They would give you the chance to easily see the data that is collected about you. You could correct it if it's wrong. You could remove it if you like. But that doesn't solve the question of how social media sites can operate if they aren't able to sell ads based on troves of user data.

The obvious answer is to make social media a subscription service. Users would pay for their accounts. Not everyone would be able to afford that, and not everyone would be willing to pay. But some sites are trying out this idea. One idea is to run ads, but users can pay a fee and avoid the ads. The data on these users would not be collected. Another idea is to let

Setting an Example

Tim Cook made his famous speech about data privacy at the headquarters of the European Union. Earlier that year, the EU had enacted strong privacy regulations called the GDPR (General Data Protection Regulation). The GDPR is a sweeping set of rules and regulations. It is designed to give citizens of European Union countries more control over their personal data. It requires any company in any nation that does business with EU citizens to take certain measures to protect those people's data. It does not protect American or Canadian citizens—or anyone outside the EU. (Canada has laws similar to the GDPR, but as of this writing, they are not as strong.) Because companies like Facebook and Apple have customers all over the world, they must comply with the GDPR regulations for their European customers. Perhaps soon the United States and Canada will follow in the EU's footsteps and do more to protect their citizens' data.

If people want safe social media where they own and control their information, they may have to come up with creative solutions on their own.

individuals and small business sell products on the site in return for a small percentage of the profits. This model would not be as profitable as Facebook and Instagram, but it might be profitable enough to provide the service.

These ideas may not catch on. And it will be very hard for any site to compete with the giants: Facebook, Instagram, Snapchat, and the rest. But who knows? Better ideas will come along. People are creative. Identifying a problem and finding a way to fix it is quintessentially American. If people really think that being the product on social media is a problem, they'll likely find a better way.

Chapter Notes

Introduction

1. Monica Anderson and Jingjing Jiang, "Teens, Social Media, and Technology 2018," Pew Research Center, May 31, 2018, http://www.pewinternet.org/2018/05/31/teens-social-media-technology-2018/.

Chapter One. Who Am I?

1. Transcript of Mark Zuckerberg's Senate Hearing, *The Washington Post*, April 10, 2018, https://www.washingtonpost.com/news/the-switch/wp/2018/04/10/transcript-of-mark-zuckerbergs-senate-hearing/?utm_term=.194b8c3a9932.
2. "Media Information Kit 2018," *National Geographic Kids* magazine, https://www.nationalgeographic.com/mediakit/assets/img/downloads/2018/NGK_2018_Media_Kit.pdf.
3. *Forbes* magazine, "Print Demographics," Forbes.com, https://www.forbes.com/forbes-media/wp-content/uploads/2015/06/2016-PrintDemographics.pdf.

Chapter Two. What Do They Want?

1. Michael Patrick Lynch, *The Internet of Us* (New York, NY: Liveright, 2016), p. 90.
2. Jeffery Selingo, "How Colleges Use Big Data to Target the Students They Want," *The Atlantic*, April 11, 2017, https://www.theatlantic.com/education/archive/2017/04/how-colleges-find-their-students/522516/users-behavior/562154/.

Chapter Three. Who Are They?

1. Yael Grauer, "What Are Data Brokers and Why Are They Scooping Up Information About You?" *MotherBoard*, March 27, 2018, https://motherboard.vice.com/en_us/article/bjpx3w/what-are-data-brokers-and-how-to-stop-my-private-data-collection.
2. Andrew Prokop, "Cambridge Analytica Shutting Down: The Firm's Many Scandals Explained," *Vox*, Updated May 2, 2018, https://www.vox.com/policy-and-politics/2018/3/21/17141428/cambridge-analytica-trump-russia-mueller.

Chapter Four. Protect Yourself

1. Kalev Leetaru, "The Data Brokers So Powerful Even Facebook Bought Their Data, but They Got Me Wildly Wrong," *Forbes*, April 5, 2018, https://www.forbes.com/sites/kalevleetaru/2018/04/05/the-data-brokers-so-powerful-even-facebook-bought-their-data-but-they-got-me-wildly-wrong/.
2. Jason Cipriani, "How to Turn off Facebook's New Facial Recognition Feature," CNET, March 1, 2018, https://www.cnet.com/how-to/turn-off-facebook-facial-recogition-feature/.

Chapter Five. The Future of Privacy

1. Paul Hitlin, "Internet, social media use and device ownership in the U.S. Have Plateaued After Years of Growth," Fact Tank, News in Numbers, Pew Research Center, September 28, 2018, http://www.pewresearch.org/fact-tank/2018/09/28/internet-social-media-use-and-device-ownership-in-u-s-have-plateaued-after-years-of-growth/.
2. Jay Willis, "What the Cambridge Analytica Scandal Means for the Future of Facebook," *GQ*, March 23, 2018, https://www.gq.com/story/ari-melber-cambridge-analytica-facebook.
3. Tim Cook, Address to European Parliament Conference on Data Protection and Privacy, October 24, 2018, https://www.youtube.com/watch?v=kVhOLkIs20A.
4. Ibid.

Glossary

algorithm Steps or rules followed in an operation designed to solve a problem.

black market A place where stolen or otherwise illegal goods are bought and sold.

CEO Short for chief executive officer, the top executive of a company or non-profit institution.

data Facts and statistics collected and compiled for the purpose of research or analysis.

data broker A company or individual that collects, analyzes, and sells information.

data mining The science of examining large amounts of information to get useful facts and statistics.

media Sources of communication, such as newspapers, television, radio, and the internet.

meme An often funny photo or video that is widely shared on the internet (taken from the word memetics that refers to information that is passed culturally rather than genetically).

model A mathematical description of a system, that can result in predictions.

multinational A business, entity, or activity that operates in several different countries, or includes people from many different countries.

platform A place where a person can express his or her views and opinions.

renegotiate To try to come to a better agreement over a deal or contract.

trove A large amount of valuable objects.

Further Reading

Books

DiPiazza, Francesca Davis. *Friend Me: 600 Years of Social Networking in America*. Minneapolis, MN: Twenty-First Century Books, 2012.

Eboch, M. *Big Data and Privacy Rights*. Minneapolis, MN: Abdo, 2017.

Nieuwland, Jackson. *Coping with Social Media Anxiety*. New York, NY: Rosen, 2018.

Small, Cathleen. *Make the Most of Facebook and Other Social Media*. New York. NY: Cavendish Square, 2015.

Websites

Connect Safely

Connectsafely.org

Resources and advice for adults and teens for safely using social media and other online communications technologies.

Media Smarts

Mediasmarts.ca

Canada's center for digital and media literacy. Contains a wealth of information designed to give youth the critical thinking skills they need to be informed and engaged digital citizens.

Index